DREAMS DOWN UNDER
celebrating Australia

Jay Ramsay

KFS
NEWTON-LE-WILLOWS

Published in the United Kingdom in 2017
by The Knives Forks And Spoons Press,
51 Pipit Avenue,
Newton-le-Willows,
Merseyside,
WA12 9RG.

ISBN 978-1-909443-97-6

Copyright © Jay Ramsay, 2017.

The right of Jay Ramsay to be identified as the author of this work has been asserted by him in accordance with the Copyrights, Designs and Patents Act of 1988. All rights reserved. No part of this publication may be reproduced, stored in a retrieval system, transmitted in any form or by any means, electronic, photocopying, recording or otherwise, without prior permission of the publisher.

Acknowledgements:

The cover image is by 'Ubirr', photographed by Thomas Schoch.

LOTTERY FUNDED | Supported using public funding by **ARTS COUNCIL ENGLAND**

Table of Contents

Prelude   9

1. Outside In

    Sulphur Crested   13
    Lorekeet   14
    Bangalley Head   15
    Bilgola 1.   18
    Shell   19
    By Lake Macquarrie   20
    Koala   28
    Detour   30
    Arriving   31

2. Dreams Down Under

    Emerald Beach/Beachcombing Emerald   35
    Kangaroo   38
    Wading into Moonee Creek   41
    The Fisherman   42
    The Cave   43
    Nocturne   46
    Rainforest Fragments 1 & 2   47
    Above Tallow Beach   52
    Dawn   54
    In High Paradise   57
    Passion Fruit   60

3. Returning

Water Dragons	65
The Ghalas	66
Emu	67
Owl	68
Bilgola 2.	69
The Bridge	70

Pre & Post

EK415	75

Acknowledgements 78

for Angela, always

The poet in everyone is aboriginal
  — **Les Murray**

* * *

By singing the world into existence, he said, the Ancestors had been poets in the original sense of poesis, meaning 'creation'. No Aboriginal could conceive that the created world was in any way imperfect. His religious life had a single aim: to keep the land the way it was and should be.

  — **Bruce Chatwin, The Songlines**

* * *

For a long time I prided myself I would possess every possible country

  — **Rimbaud, Saison en Enfer (Season in Hell)**

* * *

remember

the reward is the road
and love
is the pebble in your pocket

rolling clever

  — **Carolyn Finlay, 'Cariad'**

Prelude

AUSTRALIA IN THE MIND
reading Steve Parrish

Once a rainforest, now what the earth could become

red with drought, sand heaped against blue sky

primordial shapes…huge slug-like rock creatures

Uluru returned to itself unnamed

Jim Jim Falls…its primal waterfall

the great reef stencilled in turquoise sea

great bows of unspoilt untrodden sand

desert colours mirrored in a snowbound gum tree

granite mountains from Scotland's memory

eroded dreaming shapes, one like a flying tortoise

limestone cliffs smoothed into jagged fragments

hanging pristine lakes reflecting the sky

river red gum, blue gum, manna gum, grey gum

white rocks dusted with flaming orange

white beaches like snowdrift sand

iron blood red of Shark Bay where dolphins reign

1. Outside In

SULPHUR CRESTED
Sydney

A blaze of creamy handkerchief white
as raucous as their cries, drifting across four lanes
then in among these shoreline gums in the noonday heat
as if opened out of a hat, like magic —
never seen before. Jet lagged eyes wrenched
into their left field, dove-white but crow-raw
with their yellow mohicans, emissaries
of their own light: birdsong becomes bird romping
as they gang, sailors just landing
dawn-criers, winged, dove-cockerels, cockatoos
that can peck your patio plants to bits
and be docile as doves under this rusty fig tree…
with its great spreading branches, near the end of our dream.

LOREKEET

Upside down from the veranda awning
hooked orange beak peeping over
head inverted — am I?
Those seeds you spoil him with…
then the full plumage —
flame orange breast, indigo blue head
lime green cape, beak matching breast
flipped the right way up and preening
his body on the handrail, head
half tucked under green sheen of wing before
he flies, whirrs, back up again;
and that plaintive cry
that's universal, child for parent
in any form (feline too)
and is *creature* across all divides
calling division down.

BANGALLEY HEAD

The wild sea shore is an oil painting:
a single white house with a red tiled roof
perches on the sandstone cliff high above
where the hermit (in a parallel life) lives alone

The morning sun so bright
as it streams across the sea in its path
blending with the slate grey rock it reaches
like lead, effulgent, illuminated…

A single yucca stick silhouetted
rising from its pod of leaves below
reaching up into the rarity of its blossoming
(as on Malta: Blue Grotto, by the side of the road)

Sydney like a futuristic dream
hovers over these ancient cliffs
jutting out into the sea, steeped in bush
in their own imagining...

We walk with the city behind us, no looking back.

Tell us the names of everything again
that we've never seen or heard before
in this new land of Australia
ketermina, paper bush, flag iris, banksia

Prehistoric cyclads fan under our steps
packed mud up trees clinging on like koalas
— termite's nests

And through the thin screen of bush, the cliff edge
where he proposed to you

Jay Ramsay

St Michael's Cave plunging below
the wide sea shimmering with candescence: *infinity*
of the gift of life in its dancing

In the asking, the Yes we want for it
more precious than any ring

We stand on the roof of the world
where awe is our only mooring.

Returning to the path, Indian file,
where bare feet have walked for forty thousand years

no one trying to change anything
only to live rightly within the awe

the termites still building their nests
grain by grain, as you say

if this is the way we could lean to live again
our cities alive like bread…

This gum tree blossoms its warm resinous scent
its flowers fluffy as old man's beard, but honeyed

the sweetness of what was intended
hidden under our forgetting

It takes a massive remembering
that is our disconnected Dreaming
where the green world speaks to us again;
and then it takes fire, rising inside us,
to see with eyes that have been blinded
knowing what was meant.

We are facing the city again
and we must go to it, as lightly
as we step back down the path to where
the grass reaches with its zig-zag fence

above the sea of our being, and in our blood.

BILGOLA 1.

A rectangle of lido siphoned from the sea
under the rockface with its steel netting —
safe in its shallow end and walkways in,
even in the deep end, you can touch down.

The sea breaks all around, sliding
over the rocky shelf beside, and onto the beach
where the wind stretches the flags taut in the sun.
The lunar rescue buggy waits, between them.

Three women launch forward diving into the surf
their bodies briefly backlit in transparency
as it curves its frothing edge over them...surrendered;
thighs, arms, breasts, hair, eyes smiling flung.

You plough your lane lengths for fitness' sake
you venture in with your child's first steps
you wade up to your waist, and hesitate
and all around us each wave of our lives waits

the smaller, and always unforeseen, the great.

SHELL

Speckled, splayed on the beach here
in the wet morning sunlight: the heat rising
the fine filigree dark lines
etched into its sand-yellow brightness;
three rays fanning among them
spider web, sea shell, and butterfly
hatching in the air simultaneously
and quivering there in your mind's eye

as they wait to continue the filming
three castaways in eighteenth century clothing
running past a timed explosion
as it cracks with its smoke-puff — a gunshot in Paradise —
the black 4X4 inching along beside them
all a dream forever in our minds
life after lifetime drama dissolving
as we sip cappuccinos in the shade…

BY LAKE MAQUARRIE

1. wharf

North Nord, and the waves a cold grey
wind raking over them under the cloud

— a forested island far away.

A few moored boats bobbing
yours with a blue line for a blue day.

Last strip of sunset sky — a gash
of vivid crimson pink against the grey;
a pair of birds flung black in the fading light
as if by a hand, released like a boomerang —

A band in a garage nearby
tuning up, longing to play…
adolescent-tentative. It won't quite translate.

2. woodland

We take the sandy path for an hour's peace
relieved when it becomes a real one
leading out between the trees.

Your silent steps and soft tread,
the morning light as fresh.

Shedding. Words. Layers
this gum tree with its bark
in slats all round its base, discarded

its naked skin dusted orange,
your corn gold hair in its tresses.

The silence we need
to find each other again
in otherness, beyond routine.

How we need this unknown time.

Further away, and further in
not looking behind.

Reaching the lakeside with its tiny beach
of dried brown seaweed and white clams,
you sit on a fallen tree, gazing.

A rough tarpaulin shelter among the trees above,
no one around.

Alone together in our spheres of silence,
two halves and two wholes.

I place an open shell where you've sat
winged like a butterfly.

We climb back up,
and for a moment I find your mouth.
It is enough.

The trees are singing in light
trunks all uplit…

And there among the bushes
— with your pencil sharp artist's eye —
a flash of kingfisher blue
turquoise, jewelled, vivid
wren-small, twittering and hovering

a secret revealed and concealed.

Three of them.

Two gums, one stripped one clothed
yin and yang, moon and sun.

And as we reach full circle
a white sail through the trees on the blue,
under the blue

the air charged with birdsong
as we sit on the bench and listen
where listening is all there is to do.

3. shore

Places we will never see again,
these houses on Government Road
and the track beyond them leading down
branching left, ending in wild vermilion-red flowers.

The tiny concrete water station below
graffiti-encased, its green aerial lamp post;
a bleached dead tree beside it.

Purple trumpeting bindweed in the long dewy grass;
ah yes, Morning Glory.

The lake edge lapping below.
Big fish shy from my hunter's shadow
in a wreath of twisting shadows, moving out.
Tiny sandy translucent minnows
rippling the surface the sunlight catches
its wavemarks mirrored in light lines beneath,
these lines if I could make them…

Liminal edge of being,
wavelets edging fine brown shingle
bronze-wet to dry sand as I stand, sit
breathing the water's life…

The lake expands for miles.

The speedboat crashes through the silence
in its accelerating churring of backwash —
shrill voices in a tied dinghy behind
on its umbilical thread, being given a joy ride
as the boat twists and curves, at either side —

the thrill of these creatures in their main event.

Moments later, the whole lake edge disturbed
with its incoming waves, the light's reflections blurring,
no fish to be seen —

only these two large paw prints
that stood in the dawn or early morning
before Man was awake
and came to claim his lake
against its own Dreaming — disconnected, fake.

4. on the water

By the wharf, the deceptive soft mud conceals
something your eyes would never see
if you didn't know to look — and even then
seven eighths submerged in their element
just its razor shell edge barely showing
brown, gashing open naïve bare feet.

Jay Ramsay

You pull one up and bring it over
the wings of its shell vacated
as we wait or the little steel boat to reach us.

Razor fish. The lake's own teeth.

* * *

Ferried full with food bags and cozzies
the rear of her, a climb past a ledge
and on to this spread soft seating
sun-shielded, the prow in full light
and the roof scratched white.

The lightest touch of the wheel; and the two
levers pushed forward revving the engines
into a steady forward speed, steering
by the front railing, by a piece of wire
towards Paulbar Island's packed trees.

They tried to raise emus there. Imagine
being pursued by that bulk and that beak!

* * *

You fling yourself into the water
with the fearless abandonment of spirit
that's pretending to be your body as well —
and being young, being it
like your brother, and your red-haired sister
and now your mother, and father

and you're all in the water, treading it
laughing, immersed, unthinking
as life itself in its gift to us
                        only needing
to keep breathing air to be free

to be the smiling face of the deep
thirty feet through to green misty water beneath.

White kicking fleshy legs. Plenty here to eat.

* * *

We saw one circling as we closened
golden brown, shimmering against the tree tops
and then another, a dark speck against the blue
wings spread wide, full, floating: eagle

Eagle-eyed in studied flight
then a second joining it, as they near and part
its mate, like a sign. The blue so vast
nothing winged can encompass it
only swim in its ocean of air
that is the wilderness above.

The island below. No emu now, just bush
the children are leaving for —
the treasure of all their anticipation
freed from our watchful eyes.

* * *

You talk about the woman accused of killing her own child
snatched by a dingo —

How little we see unless we see right…
How blind our eyes are
trapped in our minds.

* * *

Driving again, over towards Murray's
another boat behind us cuts through your fishing line
— or so you anticipate.

And it's brand new. Code of etiquette broken.
Reaction flares, in spite of you —
until you feel the line intact.

You let it go as quickly as a fish unhooked
steering your own action. *All good*

walking the line as it pulls
reeling it in, reeling it in
petrol, diesel, rocket fuel

* * *

The women talk, the men fish
the cricket on the radio sings

The transparent line hooked with a shrimp
disappears down into the darkness
from the spool —

The merest tug on the line is *it*
(reel it in, but not too quick...)
a tiny staring silver bream you hold
to carefully free its mouth
before tossing him back in

He'll be alright, he'll be fine
you sing as he sinks as if lifeless towards the depths,
with no memory to forget...

I let him eat the bait again
happy, as you are, to be the lake's friend.

* * *

Measuring the distance back to the wharf
to swim ashore or stay on board
as you go in to the water like a shoal —

A family of fish, safe in your breath
the water calling like the day's end
where you know your home is real

The lake its extension, a water yard
of depth leading to shallows
only fed by the sea and by everything
the water dreams as its own.

coda

You show us his mangled remains
pornographic on your mobile phone
a mess of raw disfigured flesh

Nine years old. *Shark bait.*

Meanwhile just last weekend
a hammerhead and a bull shark
nose into the neighbourhood

Whose water is it anyway?

The biggest inland lake in Australia
is after all primordial
for all its domesticated edges

and today is always the day.

Jay Ramsay

KOALA
Port Macquarrie sanctuary

A creature hardly made for this earth
or what the earth has become —
a ball of grey fur stuffed up a tree
innocence incarnate as a toy to you, but really
consigned to a hospital, enforced sanctuary
against the blind progress of the highway
as we watch, listening to his microphone monologue

The first one hiding behind his paw, overwhelmed
the second coaxed out to his bottle feed
the third…I've told you, up a tree
the fourth half-hidden behind bush leaves
his tiny black snub nose you alone see
(as if he knows you are a seven year old child)

the fifth even higher, if possible out of reach
transcending the world and our peering eyes
the sixth enthroned, contrary-wise
as if posing for the camera; well, Look At Me Now

And if Christ came back as a koala
surely she'd be Peach Miracle
burnt by the bush fire, eyes sealed shut
nose scorched pink raw, barely breathing
paws esconced in mittens…yet slowly
(with all the care that innocence needs)
eyes opening, and able to hold a leaf
new grey hair emerging like spring
able to leave her basket for a fork in the tree —

and after all that miraculous resurrection
in three long koala days, the operation

that she survived, only to die
(no one knows why) having lived her time.

And can we believe in you: can we dare to?
The tropical rain leaving us all hurrying for cover
is also our answer.

DETOUR

The detour all the way down Ocean Drive
brings us to the pelicans
where you paused spontaneously nine years ago.

Childless and footloose.

Now with your ruby and a man
you walk back to cross the road by the sandbank
wanting you to see them like you wanted your adventure.

Life, meaning it's not enough to just see it
out of a car window. Get out and walk.

Three of them floating in the estuary, their great beaks
like a dream fusion between heron and swan
taking off in unison as we closen —
landing again, settling at their distance.

We three, and them.

And your journey, back at the wheel
wondering what might happen next.
                                        Again.

ARRIVING
Emerald Beach

Thunder and lightning on the highway.
Great flashes zig-zagging from inside the cloud
as soon as seen then gone — and again —

and still the cicadas as we slowed,
insistent as a moped drone.

At Urunga, a cloud of lorekeets
squealing past overhead. Then more rain…

The miles, the all day drive blurring
as we search the darkness for a sign.

The road trains heave towards you
poised at the wheel, solid in your calm.

Finally, the turning down
as the search for the house itself begins.

Walking ahead of you in the headlights and the wet,
the mail box has the number.

With its cladding and porthole windows, it's a ship
the stairs leading to its upper deck.

Windows sealed, oven-hot —
prizing them open behind mosquito slats.

And just as we think we've arrived
climbing the final stairs to rest

there on the ceiling, black against white
the biggest spider you've ever seen.

A hand's width, splayed, then stirring.
Huntsman, hunted; hunter, haunted...

The race for a kitchen bowl, anything, but big enough
and the sieve you find as well! Tipping it
upside down, racing inside its perspex...

Step out into the garden and the rain
as far as bare feet will allow.

Launch its rightful occupant, now.

Sleep tight. Down under.

2. Dreams Down Under

EMERALD BEACH/
BEACHCOMBING EMERALD
for Kim Satchell & Irina Kuzminsky

1.

The emerald is the green
wet sand, wave-licked, sun-breaking crests
rain-spattered, warm rain feeding it

and that island like a jewel out to sea
mounted in the clasp of the glittering water.

Clear pools, rock pools, rain pools
clearing to catch the sky
the banked cloud dispersing…

The beach with its Dreaming
and coves of shells, jewelled scree;
uplands of green, after rain flowers peeping
buttercup and mustard-yellow
glinting in the grass

The cliff-edge unfenced, unfettered…
(as one beach blends into the next)

A haze of dragonflies flitting among the bushes
black and orange whirring like tiny bi-planes
millennia before flight…and one riding
on another one's back…

Dakini dragonflies!
Invisible kangaroos

Everything poised in the Dreaming
that is everywhere Sacred Land

2.

A glint of mother of pearl, its sheen scraped open; an underlayer, skin inside skin, its lined sandy brown tough exterior

Note how its lines move the other way on the inside from the exterior.

A leaf, or a wing, a glimmer as if of cuttlefish but friable and paper thin: white stained with golden yellow-brown

A natural bookmark.

Half a golden brown cowrie shell, its flare scored with worm crossings like excisions and a myriad of tiny holes. We know. Not really solid at all.

A pebble the same colour scarred and scored with a lattice of tiny white lines like a fossilized internal organ.

Exquisite tiny purple shell, its downward pointing Mound of Venus stretched as tight as lycra…a faery pubis.

Heart stone scored pure and white in its marble vein, the white standing like a cave-painted torso.

Black and gold pebble, its gold streaks like torchbeams underwater…but on closer inspection a pupil at its edge ringed with an iris (gold seen from the depth).

A flat brown stone like miles of desert, mile after mile with little change right across the interior.

No point of penetration. Only songlines cross it.

The heel of a stone set like punctuation where a foot pauses:
to listen, and to turn…every instant of navigation, intuitive
as it ever was.

Jay Ramsay

KANGAROO

1.

The longed-for sight
at the head of these wooden steps
leading up from the beach in the twilight —
and filling the sky: standing, forepaws raised
entirely in his own domain
sentinel to all that is wild
blending fawn-brown with rock and grass
deer-brown as he sees us: freezes, then shies
a few feet back into the undergrowth
covering him as if naked: and lingering there
not unduly afraid, or not of us,
in side profile: fine ears and snout…
then vanishing, apparition, as we skirt him

And nothing else like him, search as we might
over the windswept cliff grass
tracking around the bushes in motion
to where he still is, but invisible
as this world that can only grace us
at all the edges of our domination
our everywhere habitation that we call home.

He stands at its threshold. He knows.

2.

You'd glimpsed them through the bathroom window
on the other side of the lattice fencing —

Come to us! Come to civilization
grazing on the front lawn grass

in full view of where the neighbour yesterday
was slicing a corrugated metal sheet
making the most tortuous sound. Came to this
grass long before we were here. Bush clearing,
beach a few hundred hops away…

The papa sits up, forepaws, nose alert
mama chews beside the joey:
a mirror family.

We gaze at each other
across a little gap of tarmac —
here and the other side become one.

A white pickup approaches, slowing.
We wave as he passes, relieved.
They go on being.

A woman in a 4X4 smiles
dividing the distance between us.

But just then, alert to something else
he hops, they all hop, feinting sideways to the edge
and papa takes up a position on the road.

Front paws planted, tail stretched back
a dinosaur become a swan.

The vehicle approaches again: a re-run.
Standing his ground is what he does
and he can stand proud.

Mama-joey, joey-mama do their thing
all in a flowing, nose to grass

And with a swish of an invisible wand
they're all leaping and gone…

leaving us high and dry, smiling
wannabee wallabees.

3.

We climb up past them, one by one
each one stopping us in our tracks
on to the observation point, in noonday heat

and there across the gleaming green expanse
they're grazing in their own bright named grass
undisturbed, wild, forever in their own time

as Mt. Corumba rises behind them
like an extinct volcano on the skyline
before we came here…up from Eden

Man the hunter, and man the sewage outflow developer

Man the surfer in the waves below
on Shelley's Beach, acceptable

Man and woman smiling as we pass
risen from the hidden sea cave's depth

Man become poet holding this hope
of living in respect, and not ego

nor false transcendence either
fat and holy and holding a mobile phone

barely deigning to look at the ground…

We hold this vision, as we are held in the sun.

WADING INTO MOONEE CREEK

Remove shoes.
Kiss mud with feet
(cool out of the heat).
Notice exquisite oyster shells
fossilized into slate dark rock beside.
Wonder: how many feet?

The river stretches, across the sunlit sand
to where it meets the sea.

It seems shallow enough.
Its current swirls.

Soft branches of tamarisk trees.
Mother place.

Wade in, not sure of what you will find
(sand, worm holes, then water blurring)
or how deep.

She thinks it will be just too deep
(it all depends on the tide)
She woman. She mother. She right.

THE FISHERMAN

He's there as we take our twilight beach walk
rod vertical in the sand, and the line stretching
invisibly into the incoming waves —
on a little garden chair, as I ask him
What are you hoping for? like a question of life
Just a fish, mate! he's saying, smiling
alive to the metaphor
What sort of fish?
Oh, it could be a bream or a whiting
I don't know, I haven't even had a bite yet
I could be here until 10 o'clock at least...
but I can always look at the waves
— which is not a bad pastime, I guess...
And we're both smiling as I touch him
lightly on the shoulder with my hand-held shoes
in the same kingdom of surrender
where all I have is this gift for you.

*　*　*

The ceaseless suck and hiss of the waves
and the lighthouse beyond flickering on the island
Oh to sleep on the beach, you say —
and I want to, like the waves want to break.

THE CAVE
for Kim

Descending this steep green spur of grass
to what seems inaccessible — the rocks below
jagged as they are deep, igneous, scarred
black under the hot mid-afternoon sun

and this thin crumbling path
of tiny scree inside the grass...

The sea below, redoubled in sound
ears, eyes cocked for the tide
...this is no place to drown.

The opening in the cliff face over to the left
invisible from the grassland edge
a tall vertical gash in the stone

And step by step over sharp ridged rock
and bladderwrack slippery to the stance
each conscious step towards where you're going

Then it opens,
full-throated...and the undersea rock
an unexpected rose-pink
the water inside running crystal clear
among tiny fish, and sunken spread starfish,
the light rippling up into its eaves, walls
the almost smoky light reflected from the water
light as your figure from behind as you enter in,
as light entering darkness —

Then it opens deeper
extending towards its full length in this passage
submerged beyond the soft sandy pool where you stand
up to your knees, waiting...

the sunlight through it glaring like a torchbeam
and with each wave breaking, a long ripple of water
coursing back into the cave mouth and its running chamber

a low-slung ripple, like an eel
a big black submerged eel you imagine there
in the darkness where your eyes can't penetrate
— a whiplash of sensing, smelling your own fear —

And the intuition to go in further
to wade in, to swim, to crawl
all along its length and be born, reborn

the light at the end of its tunnel a strange sun
where it hovers in a parallel dream
as you drift out leaving your body behind
drawn inextricably towards it...

lingering, as each ripple breaks in
glad of the cool out of the beating sun's heat
you pause between light and dark, being and immersion
above and below...in two directions

Being born, reborn
primordial as these walls
light-painted with their shapes
as at Lascaux or Chevet, but timeless
abstract as desire itself in motion
as my longing for the depth of you
parting your hair, licking your tender fruit
before my tongue reaches through
and your water comes to meet me...

Mother cave then, in Man Place
lover cave for lovers of life
little fish and starfish
and your child's fear in its depths
that each rippling wave washes away
until there's none of it left...

only the cave, this nameless sea-cave place, and you

ready for the light beyond again
that is the other side, here.

coda

Emerging, you find it
in a cleft in the rock —
wedged solid to your prying fingers:
a shell sea-worn to pearl
mother of pearl, silver and shining
for centuries...and today.

NOCTURNE

The wind that is the sea's white cresting breaking waves
blown inland from the beach.

The possum that is busily scratching for his own reason on
the roof.

A deep sighing in the dark as something completely unnamed
entered the space of our room.

The copper snake silent as R.E.M. sleep under the wooden
slats of the house.

The fridge coming on with its soft electric hum
not expecting anyone to hear it.

Your breath as you turn, naked in our twisted
single double almost redundant sheet.

My bare feet on the stairs, reaching you.

RAINFOREST FRAGMENTS

1. Dorrigo

Stepping in out of the sunlight and out of time into its dewy cool mountain depth

— trees soaring, packed close, greenly intertwined…my whole skin alert, the path soaked red.

Closer to trees than I've ever been
in this moistening of skin to air to skin

The path reaches in.

We pass under its overhang of branches, and enter its steep-sided cathedral

its pillars these carrabeen trees with their splayed rooted trunks reaching ever deeper as they rise, draped in tresses of green leaf creeper

— giant as redwoods, where red cedars were —

And what has fallen lies where it fell, moss-covered among green palm and lily leaves.

The thin tarmac path keeps us on track. Imagine it pathless.

You worry about leeches.

And the palms blossom blood red with their pendants of berries.

And this hollow carrabeen like an invitation to step within
and close your eyes.

(A giant orb at chest height).

Saplings and fallen logs and underbrush all intertwined.

The trees stand tall like a tribe.

One leaf on the path is all it takes. You lift its largeness to
exclaim it, and something bites from its underside — like a
needle penetrating your skin.

You can't see what it is.

The whipper bird's echoing lash of single-noted song we
were mimicking…

P—ciao!

The rainforest bites…pin-prick initiate.

And this hollow trunk with its leafmould and green shoots is
open like a womb.

The sun slowly breaks in, and the cathedral is dappled
emerald.

A small waterfall reaches the path, continuing under it, and
its rock pool meniscus is alive with small scudding beetles.

We're on the Waterfall Way. You begin to hear its closening
roar through the trees.

At some point you get the same invisible pinprick, and I'm
reaching for the ointment.

The path steepens.

A slatted suspended wooden bridge spans the outflow…as you walk to its centre, your feet bouncing as it moves.

Then the waterfall, a pouring white ribbon plummeting into its plunge pool…and you can walk around behind it where the cliff's underside shelves in a shallow cave.

This is how it was before the bridge.

How many people have stood here across time?

The cave ceiling drips, and the fine spray from the curtain of falling water blows back towards you like a balm.

Curtain of green hanging leaves between.

Curtain of your closed eyes.

On the walk back, all I remember is the moment I left the path and walked in among the bushes and briefly out of sight as I'd been longing to.

Fungus stepped up a dark brown tree like a totem.

The skeleton of that same leaf on the tarmac, stripped to its veins.

The rain birthing and recycling everything.

2. Woolgoolga

We cross a symbolic ford through a sunken stream, all four wheels of the vehicle as if cleansed.

This time, no tarmac path. This time, it is crossing a series of streams, having to become present to each slippery stone step.

Your footwear is not the best.

A pudenda shaped pool of gleaming brown water in the mud, birthplace of mozzies, Aussies, and us.

A path lit by morning sun become another stream among the trees. Stream paths criss-crossing ours, not us.

Forest floor art: the husk of a palm leaf, hollowed out, among fallen ruby red leaves and yellowing green, straw fragments. Canvas of mud.

Bright red and blue, electric blue. Kingfisher blue berries as if dropped from an invisible broken necklace.

When the leech strikes curving and bending on your tiny brown leg, you scream in momentary panic. My fingers pluck it off quicker than salt or fire.

Lianas on the path as you laugh about Tarzan and Jane. You rest on one for a swing, just your size.

You walk on ahead, the colours of your T shirt blending perfectly to green striped rain…shorts and bare legs, head and long wet side-parted matted hair slightly bowed. The present walking towards the future.

A threshold marked by two dead palm leaves leading to a fallen tree we have to stoop under. Rainforest Passover.

A decapitated rhino beetle surrounded by ants.

Tiny wild flowers and vast soaring trees. Extremes.

The light on the water like mist, but electric, an otherwordly sheen.

A clearing of soaring ghost grey gums. The haunted green.

This bridge is a wreck of twisted blue metal, rudely pushed aside by the foaming flooding water.

Why did they even need to build it?

The old crossing, a large flat stone slab (like a standing stone) completely undisturbed and adequate.

This waterfall, three ribbons at the grey cliff's edge...the water listening whispering all the way down onto the horizontal outflow of the rocks beneath.

What is man-made here is not blessed, it is rusting, abandoned, finally inconsequential (no sequence, no linear meaning).

You carry back a fan of found leaves in your hand, even as your shoes weep their leather stain.

Four times the leeches come for your bared ballerina flesh.

The last one is his, however, undetected until we stop for lunch back in civilization where he plucks it from his ankle for our gaze...and it lies there twisting on the hot tarmac, engorged with its fill of blood.

Jay Ramsay

ABOVE TALLOW BEACH
Byron Bay

The high moment, unforeseen, which gathers everything
this great open bow of sulphur-white sand
jade-turquoise sea edging in for miles
for as far as we can see
the bush green-dark behind reaching the beach
the lighthouse just behind sparkling in full sun
risen white above its castellated base
without need of flame — the sand shimmering…

and all these tiny figures in the sea's swell
as each rising wave inches surfing towards them
seen from above — that's us

so small, and so held
in this invisible sea-air palm
that is, and is not, and is
this round of sky sea sand sun
this paradise of a day that is our lives
bright as they can be in their created being
at play…like Newton's child
holding a sea shell to his ear
on the shores of infinity…as each wave breaks silently
flattening out in its slowly seeping white surf

that is you,
camera poised in hand
from your extended arm —
angelic witness and woman
as we stand on our mountain
that is love for all of this
sheer *heart-delighting light*
as essential Byron phrased it

of bodies, lives, surrounded by light
flames, faces, all becoming light

hearts alive with light becoming eyes
lips, smiling, streaming

held in exquisite form, beauty
deep in the harmonics of Light

Jay Ramsay

DAWN
for Jag

The impulse of dawn that begins
from an energy deep in your body
flexed like a bow-string —
to be fresh, alive, ahead of your life.

Your soft insistent knock on our door
to leave in ten minutes.

The banked cloud rising over the sea
still grey and lightening: orange fire-strips
gleaming above it…and then the sun.

The beach a slowly waking liminal pavement
walkers, cyclists, surfers all
in the first silence of the day's beginning
spacious with courtesy.

So our sun rises.

One spontaneous exchange, though
about a large fish left stranded, gutted
half-covered in sand, staring in its air death
washed in by the tide? Landed here?

We can only surmise.
It echoes there, like a night dream
a fact that's unexplained.

The channel stream between the stillness of sand
to our crossing — its low bank curving inwards,
a crab in its flow caught by the sun
white shell and red antennae reaching.

Another, hermetic in a hole
a trussed bundle of retreating legs.

The tea tree lake reaches inwards
as we follow the course of its stream
towards the edge of trees.

The Woman Place draws us in.

Tea tree, its water stained bronze
as a Scots burn…but darker
a varnished brown

the lake round its corner.

At the trees' edge, its reflections deepen
the water burnished brown-gold now
from the branches lit by the sun —

mud bank ooze and blue sky combined
branches multiplied in water,
shimmering between solid and liquid,
painted as if in crystal…primordial.

The lake expanding quietly beyond
this other lake, where we pause
and no speed boats come…

These birds' webbed feet
hieroglyphic in the sand
runic, ever-dissolving…

These branches golden and blending
light with shadow *where light is its shadow*
reflecting a brief scintilla of rainbow

And this blue tent pitched deep among the trees
where the tribe lived; our feet bare
as we step in over its foliage
pricking their skin awake.

Someone in the tent maybe still dreaming?
Its zipped cocoon.

Something not ready to be seen.

Meanwhile the outflow soaked with dawn light
bronze, orange, golden — on fire —
menstrual in its intensity.

Only one thing left to do: swim.

IN HIGH PARADISE
for A., A. & A.

A green road out there in the sun
through small towns, then near empty valleys —
Nimbin Rock like a craggy phallus protruding into the blue;

And Nimbin, the Wild West town
where all the cowboys are green too…
a rainbow-painted fence in front of one of the houses.

Through towards the Caldera, higher, where you are;
your driveway telling us *By Invitation Only* —
a winding dirt track surrounded by beauty
a handful of parked vehicles in the shade.

Your house open at all its edges like your heart
with its front and back veranda, the light beating down
among tall gums, palms, bananas
everywhere a vivid almost unearthly green,
and earthy as the day.

You sit and roll some grass, homemade
the longed-for coffee busy percolating
leaving the children to play upstairs with a ball
great, blue and round as the sky.

No one obliged to do anything.

Your fridge says *Magic Happens*, that simple
and 'wanted, meaningful overnight relationship'
your To Do list as continual for your estate.

Spotty the black dog lies panting in the sun.

You dribble and knee a football, from your previous life
returning home soon to your ailing mother…
the light etches your life.

You sit watching under this spreading fig
its grey branches and leaves alive with light,
as you smoke, a mellifluous rarity.

What is your life here? Being
all we long to quietly be
beyond the hurrying, driven fantasy

Paradise of Being, freed
— all metaphor, without an agenda —
in each day's unfolding…

And all afternoon, beings appearing
as if by magic floating in, relaxed, sun-kissed
as if dreamt by the light into being
in their metaphysical outline

As we sit and scoop out passion fruit
and all I can think of is yours
and how it is, down under, with you

As you then chance by, walking quietly past
just as I'm reciting poetry, as I ask
if you might join us and listen
on a *chez longue* already waiting

The light between us as palpable
as my enunciation — leaping
the small distance between our eyes
the words understood as soon as spoken
in all their intention. Paradise of listening,
your understanding a suspended smile

And when you stand to revisit your car
the light drenching you, shining through your skirt,
transparent to your thighs —
spiritual, sensual, sexual with light;

two guys mock-fighting with tepee poles
tilting and leaning, in straw hat and sarong!
Nothing can go against this light,
its purpose as strong.

The same faith as your hands on the drum
letting the rhythm hold you
realizing you can, and smiling

The others below, swimming in the pond
(inflatable dinghy upturned, laughing...)

The Sphinx above in the eyeline of rock horizon
traced against the blue, clothed in treetops,
inscrutable as She ever was.

Poignant as our leaving, then, unknowing of our return
this moment, this afternoon only, like life
'this day that will never come again', as you said
precisely like it has —

and the threads like filaments reaching between us
as strongly scored
as only music can ever be, in ether
between our hearts as we stand and linger...

the threads that will reach
across all distance, and in between
like the light that holds us, as invisibly
above each location of our lives

— and as we each travel home, letting go.

PASSION FRUIT

1.

First thing you showed us as we arrived
in your peaked cap and faded damson red shirt,
shorts and bare feet, just off your skateboard
with your surfer's innate balance
                              Here, try this!

just plucked from the Tree of Life
with its rainforest green skin and stalk
as you nipped off the top of it like an egg
and said *Here, suck it!* We all did —
even as you had the knack
so it stayed half-eaten, in its
infused seeded gold secretion

And now we're up in High Paradise
(near the Blue Nob, within sight of the Sphinx)
you have a bowl full of them in the kitchen shade
their skins wrinkled as you laugh about how
despite age, they can actually be tastier…
as I slice one in half now, and we
tease it out with two teaspoons;
our eyes meeting —

And a little later as we kiss, I whisper to you
about your paradise fruit, and all that hot afternoon
all I can think of is seeing it open
and slowly smearing it over your lips
and running my tongue down to lick out its sweetness,
with you its fruit.

2.

Absolute ripeness: your cunt running with juices
over my fingers cupped between your cheeks;
and from it, scooped like some otherworldly semen
onto your pubis...with the wind and rain
beating outside on the roof, your daughter asleep
as suddenly, as if by a spell
leaving us to candlelight and the night, the longest night
that is ours, thrust after thrust in its surrender
only getting closer...*and still light years*
of lovemaking between us...imagine:
before we will be consumed in You.

3. Returning

WATER DRAGONS

There, below the decking at this stop by the river
underneath all our civilized cappucinos
perfectly blended in with the dappled shade
on the rocks and patchy grass above the water,
these lizards that you'd told us about
by a swimming pool in one of your gardens
water dragons: but not the least bit aquatic
so dry as they sit up in the heat: small foreclaws
and long whiplash length tails: they look up
toward us with hopeful anticipation
at the railing above, of something to eat —
and we have nothing, only a few crumbs
and that's enough to send them scurrying
back and forth…a few grains of sugar, too
licked by their darting tongues…little
dragon dinosaurs in miniature, with no sound,
fast as passing flies, still as stone
here at the foundations where we have no home
only the miles of highway to come;
humanity's endless evolving road.

THE GHALAS

Ah, the ghalas…and here they are
pecking in the grass at the base of a Norfolk pine
like a landed cloud of pigeons, but with these
pink ruffs that make them, you know, a bit special —
landed on earth from elsewhere, like all birds,
and as all birds should be seen
in the delight of our eyes,

in our own freedom.

EMU

With its orange eye in profile, duck's beak
and duckling fluff reaching down its neck
you'd never guess at the power of what's below:
a vast fluffed-out midriff on legs
poised for any predator, for pursuit;
antithesis of ostrich, making you glad
she's on the other side of the fence
with kangaroo and wallaby, in among the trees
while she lingers here, right on the edge
of where we're walking, ready to peck
at any offered scrap of your flesh!

Jay Ramsay

OWL

Yellow-eyed frog whisperer, if that's who you are
hawk-eyed in your downy grey-speckled coat
perched on the slow swing release bar
of the door frame, right in our path
between two sections of this sanctuary —
and not giving an inch in your gaze
so we can just swish past
and not notice you…so you step slowly forwards
prizing the door a crack as we file close behind you
(a couple on the other side too nervous to proceed)
and you, what do you do? Secure on your perch
forever here first, you merely glance down
as if at the traffic passing under a bridge.

BILGOLA 2.

From high flight to landing…a spread-eagled
white and turquoise wing speck in the blue
high above the beach, and some way out to sea
where the thermals have carried you

where edge is all you are: air, apostrophe, awareness
flying man — and how steering is air-knowing
between how you can soar and how you can drift dangerously
off course, with your bird's eyes for waves like a surfer's
but invisible, meteorology of the moment —

We watch you finally come in, slowly descending
in your harness and triangular light steel frame
metre by metre to a perfect practised soft
landing in the sand — you make it look easy

and it's years in the air, you will tell me
about the knowledge you need to fly and be free, to make
Leonardo's dream a reality, defying gravity
where the key is lightness, updraught, carrying you

a feather in the breath of God; as improbably
as we already are and one day will be.

Jay Ramsay

THE BRIDGE
in memoriam Edward Albert Wray, 1884-1929

1.

Into the past, where nothing exists:
a gap called grandfather
until years later your letter arrives, uncle
sent via Australia —
and here he is, or rumour of him
nicknamed 'Prince' (or Ted to some)
a stonemason first, who dug for the dead
like his famous father, in Blackpool
and then an engineer who laboured
in the Valley of Shadow, for its entrails
— designing the first sliding doors for the tubes —
and then tendering for...The Bridge.

Drank, never drove, was overweight, died
on board ship from Melbourne to Brisbane.
Was only 45. Heart attack. Was separated
or seemingly, from my glamour-loving grandmother
who was in England at the time —
no one quite seems sure why.

No further facts. Unbridgeable.
His dream for Sydney and Perth still floating
in the ether for another life, unrealized.

One day his photograph arrives
out of the blue, unasked for —
and here he is, standing tall
in a three piece tweed suit
breasted with fob watch chain
tight tied tie, handkerchief loose

poking from the left lapel pocket;
close short hair, high domed forehead
and a smile as wide and as warm as the sun
greeting me across seventy years
out of time, and beyond.

One smile, one face (same nose as mine!)
one blessing, for life in spite
of the darkness: this love, its light
a piece of the jigsaw restored,
a piece of my life. And his gift
in the dream of my own

to build a bridge between the worlds,
to tell the story of our Return
to make it a monument: great as it is, like stone
in ether: the air of all our becoming
finding the one journey that has meaning
which is God finding us finding God
in our own soul.

2.

We take the ferry from Manly, it takes us
out into the open sea under grey cloud
after all this bright sun: past buoys and bush edge
with the dream of Sydney rising beyond
in its angular jagged skyscrapers:
the future that is come. How many dreamings
how many designs, all reaching taller like Babel,
tier after tier, made this? And all
its unmaking too, transcending nothing
unmasked to its monetary bubble, the world's
as fragile as it is crazy to bursting...
twin towers falling, Babel itself
leaning like Pisa to the one
language that can redeem us?

But the bridge remains...as we round the bay
a motor launch just ahead of us
in its curving path of foam...and there it is,
sombre as the day, huge as the Industrial Revolution;
dark iron spanning the water, its curve upheld
by each thick suspended thread; and in its meshed centre
you climbed to fearlessly on its walkway of air —
twin flags, too tiny to make out
and all the harbour around and beneath it.

Was this your dream? You didn't live to see it
while it spans time, like your face meeting mine
and for two or three hours it is ours in the sun
across the glittering water, as the day clears
as we stroll between it and the Opera House
rising like a shell cluster out of the sea
bearing an invisible Aphrodite —
transient as we are, and gladly
to live this green day with love
being monument enough
and more than enough
for our dream...

And here you are, grandfather, still smiling
as your eyes seem to say only
Dear boy, love is all it means.

Pre & Post

EK415

The illuminated computer plane moves slowly across the globe.
We leave at 8 in the evening: in Dubai it's now 8 a.m.
however in Sydney it's 3.27 the following morning…
Your head just can't get round it, your mind slips
you abandon time for these waves of darkness
that return as waves of involuntary sleep.
Nothing, after all, is in your hands.

And we leave time zones as we do each other
facing forwards, needing to adjust our watches
local time always our rational priority.
But love has no watch, love is out of time
catching fire with its flashback memories, its thread
eternally weaving between past and future,
necessitating Now. You are my time
asleep, awake, in your own life like your headset
leaning back in the seat beside me —

always travelling towards our final destination.